Fifty
Biggar Little Poems

Andrew McCallum

Biggar Little Festival
2011

Published by White Craw Publishing
14, Boghall Park, Biggar, ML12 6EY

Copyright © Andrew McCallum 2011

www.andrewmccallum.weebly.com

All rights reserved

ISBN 978-1-4478-5973-4

Typeset in Georgia
Printed by Antony Rowe, Eastbourne, East Sussex.

Brownsbank Cottage

A breath of wind catches in the gean-tree,
fluttering the dry leaves and the small change of the sun,
and it seems for a moment that the light is whispering.

There are ghosts in this place.
They are to be heard in the mouse-scratchings,
the seedpods cracking in the tindered broom,
the suck of the draught beneath the kitchen door.

The Grieves still move through these two rooms
in slow mutual orbits, with no need for words,
familiar and comfortable in their companionship;
two chittering lights, fingering the relics of their lives
and touching lightly the lingering echoes of the
laughter and the poetry with which the silence thrums.

And on such an evening as this,
when we have silence yet over the Border hills,
and the gloaming gathers close about the door,
on the doorstep his voice still softly sings:

The rose of all the world is not for me...

Cinq Cinqain on Biggar Pond

Today
the boating pond
is almost deserted;
only the waterbirds remain
this late.

A breeze
combs the surface,
teasing out its tresses
in rippling waves across the pond's
mirror.

Two swans,
staid and stately,
sail seven seas among
a busy harbourful of ducks
and gulls;

strung out
in their wakes bob
a squadron of cygnets,
fully grown but still moulting brown
and grey.

The trees
on the south bank
nod their heavy shadows
low over their own reflections,
sun-spent.

renga from whitecastle hill

1
brand new light crinkles
like cellophane on the fields
wakening the birds

2
scarves of mist muffle
the neck of Whitecastle Hill
a curlew beckons

3
latches click, doors close
figures move upon the land
singly, intently

4
the sky is the bright
iris of a peacock's eye
wide and unblinking

5
starlings swoop and swirl
in a curling wisp of smoke
slowly dispersing

6
the sunlight settles
in a lawnchair and watches
its shadows playing

7
the sky expands and
deepens as the earth contracts
hunching its shoulders

8
the setting sun slides
its knife between cloud and earth
releasing a skylark

9
the peacock swells and
spreads a tail of stars across
the darkening sky

10
midnight comes and sweeps
the valley clean with its broom
moonlight laves the earth

Brownsbank Cottage, Midsummer Night
(for Josephine and the two Junes)

>We forget the time,
>it is still so light as we
>stand here talking yet.
>
>Through half-open eyes
>the world takes our measure,
>wishing us asleep.
>The trees have drawn their
>shades and turned the sky's blue
>flame down to a peep,
>and what dark there is
>hangs strawberry nets over
>the still quick colours.
>
>There is the silence
>besides, deeper than the dusk,
>sharper than the stars,
>that loudens our voices,
>more clearly enunciates
>the words we exchange.
>
>We speak in murmurs;
>yet still the night growls at us
>to keep the noise down.

little mitchellwood

     letting the deed shaw in clearing and copse
     the sunlight sings of a loving labour
          lilting the seedheads
          echoing birdsong

     it is we who make the woods in which we dwell
     through the love with which we
          bear its trugs of light
          hand-crumble its soil
     enlacing them with lillikines of leaf
          long limbs of poetry
          our solicitude

     wind trembles the green of little mitchellwood
     dappling the air with whispers

full moon on a cloudy night

    the lamp is smoking
    beclouding its own brightness
    it needs to be trimmed

    who can trim the moon?
    its gladness is unbounded
    it has seen the sun

l'écosse profonde

cow breath
creak and clump of cloven toe
hay spun into circular brochs
crow cough of l'écosse profonde

    a mythical place that exists only in
    the eye of its inhabitants

    a place of recursive atavism
    a den of fertility

    a beggaring of history
where death and lovemaking still take place
according to mesolithic ritual

where people drench the earth with
the sweat of their days
before returning to invisibility

haiku #1

a soft fine drizzle...
why sic a pleuter o wurds
when *smirrnin* wad dae?

Hazelnut Shells
(for TW)

>It is as far as I can reach,
>this terrace where you sat,
>munching hazelnuts,
>and watched the river thread
>its sinew through the Pentlands' eye.
>
>Your look as raw and hard as stone
>saw this sky, these hills; this
>wind lifted your hair
>and brought to your nostrils
>these scents of water and of earth.
>
>Eight millennia between us;
>yet shoulder to shoulder
>in the same land we sit,
>you feasting on hazelnuts,
>me picking up your discarded shells.

haiku #2
(for PS)

       scent of mint
                   table
     spread
          and lacking only your

     fragrant dishes
                  joy!

Fog

A flock of geese graze a fallow field,
elbowing aside slick coal crows;
the fog swallows everything in its path.

Yesterday it pressed against my window,
an unexpected visitor
waiting politely on the threshhold.
Today it does not meet me on the hill
but lies claimed by the valley.

Soon it will lift,
opening to expose the fertile earth,
whose raked grooves of raw sienna
cleanly divide balks of woodland,
the knowes kissing where they meet
at their lowest points.

poesis

    the nodding of my rowan tree
    bespeaks the blowing of the wind
    which otherwise I cannot see

Castle Hill, Symington
(for LB)

There is nothing to be seen of the iron age fort
that once kinged this castle,
but some half-dissolved earthworks
smothered by turf
and melting over the crown of the hill;
even the dirty wee rascal,
who haunts your visits here
and runs to you with the tale of his life,
is only a stumble in time
that you catch and steady
and keep from falling out of memory.

There is significance surely in the fact that
it is a child who scrambles over these ramparts,
preferring to their refuge
the sanctuary of a mother's eye;
an iron age child,
into whose waiting you are at last delivered
as he greets your homecoming.

haiku #3

rain on a puddle
its drops casting second thoughts
back towards the sky

By the White Loch

The autumn wind crackles cold
in reeds stood grey in the failing light;
a heron rises and sets off homeward.

Standing alone, resting on the shore,
an old man feels the wind in his face,
the coming night, the snow that will fall.

From shadowed shore he looks west to where,
between cloudbank and loch, a lit strip
of kame field gleams warm yet in the dusk,
golden as a dream, as creation.

He holds this image fixed in his mind,
thinks of his time, of his good full years,
watches the gold pale, watches it fade,
turns, sniffs and spits, and sets off homeward.

outside st mary's
(for TR)

    wednesday nights
    choir practice
    stained glass without god
    love without the word to weigh it down
    wind in the trees coaxing leaves to life
    branches swaying
    cradling the light

    is this the holy spirit?
    so delicate that
    those who hold it cannot feel its weight?

    it is wind and colour, tree and kirk
    given breath like art and love
    as real as brick and glass
    as voices singing
    light splashing limbs
    wind riffling leaves

midsummer, when dusk overtakes the dawn

a throstle is tapping a stone with
a snail-shell in its beak
a gowdspink hangs from a rasp
until the stem breaks

no waking-song has begun
yet the birds squabble and hurry
and huddle in the hedge's gloom
as an owl flies home

Raven

When he flies, he flies through solitude,
as through a hollow within a hollow,
which escorts him, perpetually recreating itself.

When he swoops, his wings imitate
the voice of the wind, of a scythe.

At times he flies in twos. Even then
his flight is but a falling into circles of solitude.
They maintain a quiet distance.
Their wings do not touch.
They fly in the space of two circles.

He sings in three ways, in three distinctive tongues.
All three are meant only for himself,
for his ear, for conversations with himself.

No mimic, this bird. If he speaks,
he echoes only himself, his voice
an intricate language of curved calls.

And when he flies low,
a black defiance glimmers on his wings.

Overburns

"All along the Upper Clyde, quarries pit the landscape; holes gouged by fingers from the earth."

Dorothy Wordsworth

    Pelt-bent neolith, quarryman,
    hunched in the deepening cavity,
    burning a clod of fat to guide you to the face:
    before you, the blood-smell of antler and scapula
    scraping chert from ancient sediments;
    behind you, nine heads gifted to death,
    a phallus for the fertile tap-root.
    A planet's gravity presses down on your descent.
    Your ribs are streaked with mud and silicate.

    All day long you haggle with devils, quarryman,
    for blades buried deep in the clatter of river-slag,
    until dust-drunk and sun-starved you rise
    to a birch-brushed sky, to the comfort of air,
    to the sound of hammerstone and trade.

pastoral

new grass
new lambs eating the grass
new calves butting heads under
the slow gaze of a bull beyond a wire fence
sparrows flying with pieces of straw in their beaks
seagulls
dozens of miles from the sea
eating worms turned up by the plough
the earth itself

but it is not enough
I go into the house and put on some music
I listen to violins and oboes
former trees pretending to be winds, birds and burns
listen to drums
the hides of animals
trying to be thunder

and it all works somehow
outside the earth is being lifted
rising out of itself
trees wave their arms like mad conductors
the sky breaks into applause

birthwood

    I pick up a stoat's skull
    and hold it to my ear

    in its empty chambers
    I hear not the sea but
    the wind in the top nest
    of a tall smooth-shining
    beech tree…

              …snake-whistling

apocalyptica's *farewell*

across kirkwaa
a boat
rowing out at break of day
leaving no trace behind

cille bheagha
an echo
resounding through chapelgill
and on up into an empty sky

Easter...

the flinty boned season,
through which the wind whistles
and scours the remnant rags of flesh
from this sheep's carcass,
leaving its sticks bleached clean
and white on the gnawed grass.

There can be nothing more
utterly dead than this,
this filigree of bone beneath
a sky flaking sleet
and three trees naked
on the crest of Pyatknowe.

Yet already the grass
loops strong pulling-stitches
around its ribs, while a gowan
peeks a timid eye
through the empty socket
and the trees bud beads of blood.

haiku #4

a sudden snow shower
steals from st mary's churchyard
the names of the dead

The May

Hush-a-by baby on the tree top
When the wind blows the cradle will rock
When the bough breaks the cradle will fall
Down tumbles baby, cradle and all

Mother Goose's Melody (1781)

We sat still and silent
under the silvery humming trees.

Then an elder spoke up, telling us
to go home and fetch cradles
and hang them from the boughs:

It is the May already;
swallows twine their ribbons across the sky.

Our village has stood a long time – as it always has,
the wheat has sprouted green – as it always has,
and men have died – as they always have.

Now is the time. The nights grow light.
The women sigh as they turn in their sleep,
and the birch trees' silver boughs
are lit with anticipation.

hiring fair

    my grandfather should have acted then
    stirred a swarm at the hiring fair
    by dancing his crow dance in his nicky tams
    his seckie flapping in gusts of fury
    his toothless beak   cacking
                               cacking
                               cacking
    till it made a mad murder of all the servants

    then they would have descended on the farms
    seized the means of production
    hammered ploughshares into halberds
    pitchforks into pikes
    sickles into scimitars
    cut the throats of the beefy farmers
    tupped their daughters
    and levelled the enclosures
    turning parks into riggs again

    then in his last days
    my grandfather could have hirpled to market
    a free man, a *haill* man,
    redeemed from all the flatbeds and four-by-fours
    that clog its gaits

medwyn below greenshields

grinding age-old stone
into ever finer tilth
the medwyn quarries

in deep narrow cuts
it sifts through silt with its spade
searching for something

we have built this bridge
over its labouring back
from which we can watch

but the river is
too intent in its seeking
to *tak tent* of us

haiku #5

swans crowd the pondside
a classroom of upraised hands
clamouring for bread

smiddy

    he bit on his pipe
    and smoked long round vowels
    through lips   fixed in the thinnest of scribbles
              that gripped each word in tongs
              once found in the smithies where his
              consonants were fired and burred

    in the tales he told
    he spoke of   *kye pairks*
              doors left *onsneck't*
              and men *wha'd* been gassed in the war

    his craft was mainly bicycles then
    cannibaled constructions and repairs
    but occasionally   on a fancy
                  just to entertain us
    he would fire up the cold furnace and
    spit sparks from the anvil

        then   *he's powie wad dirl as*
                  he pin't oot the airn
                  bruntin the win wi he's darg

Autumn

"... nothing but yellowed leaves bound for the earth, outside my window..."

Merle Bachman, Kentucky

Here they have all arrived at their destination
and are mulching away nicely among
the rosehips and rowan berries,
whose scarlet clusters the gales have torn from branches,
while one solitary apple clings thrawn to
my one solitary apple tree.

No frosts yet, however,
which is a worry to the village elders,
with their anxious eyes and drippy noses.

I shall go among them bearing tissues.
I shall remind them that they haven't died a winter yet,
from which thought we landward folk
can *ay tak* some consolation.

haiku #6 – gloaming

the night has risen
casting off its serpent skin
to blue the hillside

Moon Over Biggar Common

Bright moon, when was your birth?

Su Shi

    Pint glass in hand, I ask the deep blue sky,
    not knowing what year it is tonight
    beyond its sphere.

    I long to fly there on the wind,
    yet dread those crystal stars, those infinite zeros,
    freezing to death among Saturn's rings.
    Instead, I rise to dance with my pale shadow,
    better off, after all, in the world of men.

    Rounding the *Cnoc*,
    stooping to look through bedroom windows,
    the moon shines on our insomnia.
    She knows no sadness.

if I were a heron

    if I were a heron
    I would seek a mate as
    curved as I, as long of limb

    we would walk so slowly
    the fish would not suspect
    the menace of our shadow

haiku #7 – *sidhe*

    silent moving folk
    silver among the green knowes
    by sun-glinted burns

how to make a blf

take a clydesdale market town
season with people
break and blend the yolks of tradition
in a modern marinade
stir from cock-crow to owl-screech
till everyone is as dizzy as
a fast-turned fork
flash-fry some watercolours
hull some late soft flutes
infuse a jig with enthusiastic fiddles
coddle a carton of free-range actors
devil their actions
flambé their lines
add a bouquet of books
simmer gently
remove the leaves when almost done
raise the temperature to a rolling boil
dredge with anticipation

View from Knowehead Farm
(after the painting by Eileen Hood)

The hills have soaked the blueness from
the sky, and dyke and whin are bent
as memories of relentless winds.

Deep shadow-fissures split the flesh
on ancient brows and hollowed cheeks.
Snow patches liver-spot the slopes.

And here I stand on this knowe's head
in this late winter, a passing eye
through which these hills disclose themselves.

that swan is like a song with two voices

      across the pond
      in the shadow of the willows
      breast to breast with duplicity
      a swan reflects upon the solitary water
      an image of itself
      alone

      at night
      the pond is a wide and empty silence
      without imagination

manorhead
(for TB)

    it is may
    the woods brim with great splashes of
    purple white and mauve
    they shimmer in the shade
    light up thickets of ferns

    there have been rumours
    of wolves returned
    smudged tracks in the mud
    a glimpse of grey
    some wildness at the dark green core

    I cup my hands
    drink deeply
    keep looking over my shoulder
    the manor burn twists silver ropes
    coils them over rocks
    mumbles the words of its ballad
    but it will not tell me
    who has passed by
    whose footprints these are
    shining wet on the stone

Hills

Late last night
I heard a muckle noise outside my door.
Without so much as a 'by your leave'
the hills came into my house,
flinging off snow on the doorstep.

Silent and wise, without a single word,
they let it be known they had come from afar.
A few torrents tumbled down their laps,
capricious yet shy,
like laddies in awe of their grandfathers.
Wolves howled at the lampshade,
mistaking it for the moon.
A sly landslide was proffered as a hassock
as hill sheep knelt to watch the news
with its myriad murders and financial chicaneries.

Early next morning, at the cock's crow (if you will),
they departed, without farewell,
without a backward glance.
When the children came home from school that day,
I watched as they played in the moraine,
building castles that would never fall,
each stone borne up by three of its neighbours.

Crow

A sleeting wind bullies a crow.
It wobbles in the air, then berths
fully controlled on top of the tallest tree,
grinning like a jaikie being dragged off to jail,
knowing the law can no longer touch him.

Even in this godforsaken weather
the crow knows it can manage better than
those who shelter in their solid houses.
It is outside; part of God's creation,
but held by the wind in an older union.

broken bough...

    hanging year after year
    groaning in the wind
        leafless
        stripped of bark
        bare and bleached

    its song sounds harsh and thrawn
        defiant
        secretly alarmed at
        one more summer
        one more winter long

haiku #8

among fallen leaves
a butterfly, wet, windblown
seeks its lost summer

st mary's loch
(for matthew)

      a wee boy approaches the edge of the loch
      a wide selection of stones gathers
      he throws one because this is what wee boys do
           when they see a loch
             and stones waiting to be thrown
      he throws each as far as he can
      it leaves his hand in a long parabolic arc
      this happens so frequently that after a while
      the hit surface only yawns and shrugs its shoulders

      we know (with little evidence) that each hurled stone
      really does go to the bottom of the loch
      and doesn't just vanish as it strikes the water
      just as we know that a child swung above his father's head
      will return the same wee boy
      even though his feet have touched the clouds

haiku #9

walking in the woods
I lose the path, find myself
in a sunlit glade

hare
(for SL)

    skimming over the grass
    defying gravity with its joy or fear
    weight thrown off its back like water

    the sky trips over its coiling muscle
    it hurls a tunnel of space ahead of it
    the grass parts where it is yet to bounce

    the heart waits for such moments
    the pulsing blood, the weightless leap
    pushing its way through rapture

    eyes blind with ecstasy, ears set back
    our hearts too bound away
    from the tips of our grey whiskers

haiku #10

a heron flaps by
pointed bill and trailing legs
the tools of its trade

Beyond Our Thresholds

Here in the countryside, where
land enfolds water and journeying defines land's end,
we are contained by the dimensions of vision,
made tame by the breadth of the sky.

Beyond our thresholds the sky absorbs us.
We are the ascents and descents of the hillsides,
old roads that cling to skylines;
caught by the winds that stroke green fields,
the surging bores of cloud-shadow,
we mumble with the voice of journeymen,
hold horizons in our hands.

Beyond our thresholds the rain knows us,
the cornfields think about us, silos fill with grain;
and further, to where the oceans start and end,
we need not venture.

Yesterday and today, spring begins again...

Off the antlered tips of yearling trees,
the air tells you: yes, it is possible;
it can happen; there is a chance.

You stand in showers of cherry blossom
and know all your longings.
Your hands reach up, seize pieces of the sky.

A Winter's Tale

Snow still clung to the north-facing flank of the tree,
where the sun could not reach.
A thin blue shadow lay taller than the tree itself
on a satin surface of unbroken whiteness.

A crow lit nimbly on the tip of the topmost branch,
sending small clods of snow gliding to the ground.
Its black plumage shone brightly against the ice blue sky.
A dark glint of sunlight flashed from its eye.

From nowhere, a young rabbit with a broken leg
lunged fitfully through the snow.
The crow shivered out its feathers and settled down
to bide its time while the shadow lengthened.

Coulter

We made something of the valley at least,
enclosing its contours and running a
plough as best we could within their confines,
lifting slabs of ochre and tan to lay
haphazardly on strips of rough grazing.

But our labour petered out as the soil
thinned away towards the hilltops, so that
above our meagre scrapings the rock still
rises, draped in a thin mantle of green;
above that, a swirl of blue-marbled sky.

They are enough, though, to win a bite from the
indifferent hand of the wilderness,
a bield against the wind that rises white
as spume from the breaking wave of heaven:
these scratchings; this impertinence of ours.

Acknowledgements

Most of these poems appear here for the first time. However, a few have previously been published in Blast Furnace, *Both Sides of Hadrian's Wall*, *Brownsbank*, The Eildon Tree, Ereignis, IMPpress and West Goes South. 'Cinq Cinqain on Biggar Pond' was a finalist in the 2003 Ottakar's and Faber National Poetry Prize. 'haiku #1' and 'haiku #3' are two of the 'six rainy day haiku' which have been incorporated into 'Peace is a Haiku Song': a collaborative public art project between Sonia Sanchez, the City of Philadelphia Mural Arts Program and Philadelphia's First Person Arts Festival.

Thanks are due to Biggar Writers Group, whose members past and present have provided me with a valuable sounding-board for work-in-progress, and to successive Brownsbank Writing Fellows, Linda Cracknell, Tom Bryan and Carl MacDougall, for their sustaining encouragement and support.

Thanks are also due to Chris and Sue at the excellent Atkinson-Pryce Bookshop for distributing these fifty poems, and to the members of the Biggar Little Festival Committee for their tireless work throughout the year to provide an annual showcase for the work of local practitioners like myself.